COOKING THE
INDONESIAN
THE
WAY

Lerner Publications Company
A division of Lerner Publishing Group
241 First Avenue North
Minneapolis, MN 55401 U.S.A.

Website address: www.lernerbooks.com

Library of Congress Cataloging-in-Publication Data

Cornell, Kari A.
    Cooking the Indonesian way / by Kari A. Cornell and Merry Anwar.
        p.   cm. -- (Easy menu ethnic cookbooks)
    Contents: Before you begin—An Indonesian table—Soups and appetizers—Salads and side dishes—Main dishes—Desserts—Holiday and festival foods.
    ISBN: 0–8225–4127–0 (lib. bdg. : alk. paper)
    1. Cookery, Indonesian—Juvenile literature. 2. Indonesia—Social life and customs—Juvenile literature. [1. Cookery, Indonesian.] I. Anwar, Merry. II. Title.
    TX724.5.I4C68 2004
    641.59598—dc21   2003011205

Manufactured in the United States of America
1 2 3 4 5 6 – JR – 09 08 07 06 05 04

ethnic cookbooks

COOKING

culturally authentic foods

THE

including low-fat and

INDONESIAN

vegetarian recipes

WAY

Kari Cornell and Merry Anwar

Lerner Publications Company • Minneapolis

Contents

Introduction

Indonesia, a series of islands that lie in the path of countless ancient trade routes, has long reaped the rewards of its location. Over the centuries, traders from distant lands brought new religions, traditions, and recipes to the islands. The first inhabitants of Indonesia came from the Southeast Asian mainland in 2000 B.C. These people, called the Malay, introduced rice and stir-frying, a method of cooking vegetables and meats in a bowl-shaped pan called a wok.

Hundreds of years later, missionaries and merchants from India traveled to the islands of Java and Sumatra. They brought Hinduism and Buddhism along with the curry cooking tradition and turmeric, a favorite East Indian spice. Arab traders, who introduced the religion of Islam to the islands, also brought recipes for kabobs and mutton (sheep) dishes. The Europeans, mainly the Portuguese and the Dutch, contributed vegetables such as carrots and tomatoes. In return, traders took spices native to Indonesia, such as nutmeg, pepper, mace, and cloves, back to their own countries.

For a meaty, tangy appetizer, try Sweet and Sour Beef Sate with Peanut Sauce. (Recipe on pages 36–37.)

Modern Indonesian cuisine reflects the influence of all these settlers. It's difficult to name a dish that is typically Indonesian, because many favorite recipes and flavors come from other countries. The lemongrass flavoring and spicy peanut sauces featured in many Indonesian recipes, for example, have been borrowed from the cuisine of Thailand to the north. It is just this blending of flavors and traditions that makes sampling Indonesian dishes so much fun. As you try the recipes in this book, keep in mind that you are getting a taste of the countries and islands that surround Indonesia, too. As they say in Indonesia, *selamat makan*—enjoy your meal!

The Land and Its People

Millions of years ago, volcanoes beneath the ocean floor created the 17,508 islands that make up the country of Indonesia. The world's largest archipelago, or group of islands, Indonesia stretches between Australia and Asia. Its larger islands include Sumatra, Java, West Timor, Flores, Bali, Sulawesi, part of Borneo, and the western half of New Guinea. Indonesia is also made up of many smaller islands. Java is home to the capital city of Jakarta, where more than 60 percent of the country's total population lives.

The water surrounding Indonesia is as much a part of the landscape as the islands themselves. The Pacific Ocean, Indian Ocean, Arafura Sea, Java Sea, Bali Sea, Flores Sea, Timor Sea, Celebes Sea, and Sulu Sea all wash up on Indonesian shores. The first people to come to Indonesia were fishers and traders who arrived by way of these waters. Both fishing and trade still play a big part in Indonesia's culture and economy.

In contrast to the flat, deep blue expanse of the surrounding seas, many of the islands are spiked with mountains and volcanoes, including one hundred active volcanoes. The tiny island of Flores alone is home to fourteen volcanoes. The Moluccas, Indonesian islands between Sulawesi and New Guinea, are made up of very old volcanoes that have worn down over time. Black sand beaches along the coast give way to rugged mountains and lush tropical rain forests farther inland. On many of the islands, such as Java and Sumatra, farmers have carved fields into the hillsides to grow rice, a staple in the Indonesian diet. Settlers from China first planted rice on the islands thousands of years ago. Nourished by Indonesia's warm, wet climate, the crop was quick to take hold.

Indonesia is located in what is called the ever-wet zone, an area that includes land both north and south of the equator. During monsoon season, a rainy period from December to March, winds from the northwest move storm clouds across the South China Sea to the Indonesian islands. Torrents of rain fill the rice paddies. Although temperatures in Indonesia hover at about 80°F, the humidity often tops out at a sticky 100 percent. In this greenhouse-like climate, it's not just rice that thrives. Coffee, corn, soybeans, sugarcane, and tropical fruits such as coconuts, bananas, pineapples, mangoes, and papayas also grow well.

This hot island country is the fourth most populous nation in the world. Indonesia's national motto, *Bhinneka Tunggal Ika* ("They are many, they are one"), sums it up. The islands are home to people from more than three hundred ethnic groups who speak just as many languages. In 1945 the Indonesian government made Bahasa Indonesia—a language that combines elements of Malay and Javanese—the official tongue of Indonesia. But many languages and dialects are spoken on the islands. Although children learn Bahasa Indonesia in school, they often communicate at home in their parents' language.

More than half of Indonesians—including Javanese, Sundanese, and Madurese people—live on the island of Java, which accounts for less than 10 percent of the country's total land area. Java is the most heavily populated agricultural land in the world.

Life in the rural areas and villages of Indonesia has changed very little in the past one hundred years. Families typically get up at dawn and cook breakfasts of rice and vegetables, preparing the food on wood-burning stoves. Muslim Indonesians pray immediately after rising. After breakfast, children walk to school and their parents report to work in the rice fields, or *sawah*. In many areas, farmers still use oxen to plow the fields. The rice is harvested and threshed by hand and then left to dry in the sunshine. At the end of the day, children help with chores around the house. Their parents may ask them to run through the sawah to frighten away birds that eat the crops. Many villages do not have electricity or running water, and people must bathe in nearby rivers or haul water to their homes for bathing and cooking.

In Jakarta and other Indonesian cities, people generally get up early for school or work. After a breakfast of rice with a fried egg, children make their way to the bus stop or to school. Many men work on farms outside the cities. Others have business careers, or they work unloading ships at the nearest port. Although more Indonesian women have careers than in the past, many women stay home to clean, cook, and care for their families.

In the middle of the day, Indonesians with an appetite don't have to look far to satisfy their hunger. *Kaki lima* vendors (sidewalk vendors) fill the village and city streets, ringing brass bells or banging on Chinese wooden blocks to attract customers. When someone orders food, the vendor tosses a few bamboo skewers of sate on a small charcoal grill or heats a big bowl of soup. Another street food alternative is the *warung*, or food cart, which is basically a tiny restaurant on wheels. Customers take a seat at the small bench provided

A street vendor in Bali prepares sate for waiting customers.

and order a drink or whatever main dish or dessert the vendor offers. Warung vendors tend to specialize in a particular dish and are known for making some of the best food on the islands.

In the early evening, families gather for dinner, which usually includes rice, vegetables, and meat or tofu, made from soybean curd. A trip to the movies or the market or a visit with friends typically ends the day.

Regional Cooking

Some foods, such as rice, sate (grilled meat on bamboo skewers), and *gado-gado* (a salad made from potatoes, bean sprouts, cabbage, and other vegetables), are enjoyed throughout Indonesia. But most areas have their own special ways of preparing these dishes. Sate, for example, is made with different meats in different places. On the Hindu island of Bali, sate is usually made with pork, a meat that Muslims avoid for religious reasons. Throughout the islands, beef and chicken are popular choices for sate, although many Hindus choose not to eat beef for religious reasons. Traditionally the cooked pieces of meat are dipped in a peanut sauce that varies in taste and intensity depending on where it's served. On the island of Java, sugar is added to almost everything, and the sauce tends to be very sweet. In Sumatra the Minangkabau people make a very spicy peanut sauce.

Throughout Indonesia, rice is considered a symbol of bounty and is served at nearly every meal. In Java and Bali, people leave offerings of food and flowers to the rice goddess. Favorite dishes include yellow rice (rice flavored with turmeric), fried rice, and black rice pudding. In the mountains of Sumatra and the island of Madura, however, corn is the staple food. In these areas, which receive less rain than Bali, Java, and the lowlands of Sumatra do, corn is easier to grow than rice. Corn with shredded coconut and corn fritters are two popular dishes. In mountainous Irian Jaya (western New Guinea), sweet potatoes are the major crop. In the eastern part of Indonesia, a starchy food called sago forms the basis of the diet. Sago comes from the sago palm tree, and Indonesians in this region use sago flour to make a kind of sticky bread that they eat with vegetables.

Tropical fruits, including durian, mangosteen, jackfruit, salak, bananas, and coconuts, grow throughout Indonesia and have become an important part of the country's cuisine. Durian is a spiky, round, green fruit that grows on trees throughout the islands. Despite the fruit's unsavory smell (some compare it to the smell of sewage), durian's creamy white flesh is quite tasty. It is a popular snack in many Southeast Asian countries. Mangosteen has tough purple skin that protects the delicious white fruit inside. The brown skin of salak, or snake fruit, looks like snakeskin, which gives the fruit its nickname. Its crisp, light-colored flesh tastes somewhat sour. Jackfruit resembles durian on the outside but grows much larger, up to forty pounds. Indonesians eat jackfruit in two different ways. When it is ripe, they pick the fruit and eat it as a sweet snack or dessert. Unripe jackfruit is cooked with coconut milk and eaten as an entrée. Bananas of all varieties and sizes grow on the islands, and Indonesians enjoy them just as you might—as a snack or in a dessert.

Of all the fruits that grow on the islands, coconuts are probably used most often in Indonesian cuisine. The tough husk of the fruit is cracked open, and the juice is savored as a cool, sweet beverage on the steamiest of days. Coconut milk is the primary ingredient in curries, rice dishes, and desserts made all over Indonesia. Crisp, white coconut flesh also makes a delicious snack.

Holidays and Festivals

The eclectic mix of ethnicities and religions in Indonesia make for a year filled with holidays and festivals. As the descendants of Chinese,

Indian, Malaysian, Australian, Arabic, Dutch, and Portuguese settlers, modern Indonesians have combined traditions and rituals from all of these cultures to create their own unique and diverse observances. About 90 percent of Indonesians are Muslim, and Islamic holidays are the most widely celebrated.

Lebaran, the two-day feast that marks the end of Ramadan, is the largest festival of the year. During Ramadan, the ninth month of the Islamic calendar, Muslims throughout the world show their devotion to Allah (God) by praying and fasting between dawn and sunset. During Lebaran, Indonesians dress in their best jewelry and sarongs—loose, colorful garments made of a long strip of cloth wrapped around the body—and visit with relatives and friends. The crackling and popping of firecrackers give the streets a festive air as people travel from one party to the next. Along the way, they are likely to pass vendors selling *ketupat*, brightly colored rice cakes wrapped in palm leaves. Partygoers never attend a holiday gathering

Muslim women in Jakarta pray facing Mecca, Saudi Arabia, the holy city of Islam, on the first day of Lebaran, the end of Ramadan.

empty-handed—guests traditionally bring cakes and cookies to the host. The most popular dish at a Lebaran celebration is a spicy curry, featuring chicken, lamb, or beef.

The island of Bali hosts many festivals throughout the year. The night before the Hindu New Year, called Nyepi, is a great celebration. People offer gifts of meat and wine to satisfy the evil spirits that are believed to exist where two roads intersect. After dark, celebrants crowd the streets, carrying torches and banging on cymbals to frighten away any remaining spirits. Nyepi itself is a quiet day of prayer and reflection.

The grandest of all Balinese holidays is Galungan, a festival that honors the Hindu god Sanghyang Widi. Balinese Hindus believe that their ancestors return to earth during Galungan. The holiday is celebrated over three days. On the first day, people prepare religious offerings and traditional foods, such as roasted suckling pig and fresh fruits. On the second day, families go to the temple to pray, and on the third day they spend time with friends and relatives. Elaborate decorations honoring the gods and ancestors adorn roadsides, temple entrances, and homes.

All Indonesians, regardless of their religious beliefs, join together to celebrate a handful of holidays. On August 17, Independence Day, islanders commemorate the date of their independence from Dutch rule in 1945. The festivities include parades, traditional dance performances, and sporting events. Spectators may snack on sate or sip *es campur*, a fruity drink filled with a variety of ingredients, such as gelatin cubes, slices of avocado, corn, beans, bits of fruit, and shaved ice.

In August and September, after the rice harvest, Indonesians look forward to the bull races of Madura. Owners feed the bulls eggs, hot peppers, beer, and honey in preparation for the race. On the morning of the race, owners parade the decorated bulls through the island's capital city of Pamekasan before entering the stadium. Spectators cheer as they watch the jockeys, each riding on a wooden sled between two bulls, prod the animals to sprint down a 110-yard track at speeds that top thirty miles per hour.

Before You Begin

Cooking any dish, plain or fancy, is easier and more fun if you are familiar with its ingredients. The Indonesian dishes in this book make use of some ingredients you may not know. Sometimes special cookware is also used, although the recipes in this book can easily be prepared with ordinary utensils and pans.

The most important thing you need to know before you start is how to be a careful cook. On the following page, you'll find a few rules that will make your cooking experience safe, fun, and easy. Next, take a look at the "dictionary" of cooking utensils, terms, and special ingredients. You may also want to read the tips on preparing healthy, low-fat meals.

Once you've picked out a recipe to try, read through it from beginning to end. Now you are ready to shop for ingredients and to organize the cookware you will need. When you have assembled everything, you're ready to begin cooking.

Vegetable Sauté makes a healthy, low-fat main dish. (Recipe on page 51.) Serve it with a side of Thai Fragrant Rice for a deliciously filling meal! (Recipe on page 44.)

The Careful Cook

Whenever you cook, there are certain safety rules you must always keep in mind. Even experienced cooks follow these rules when they are in the kitchen.

- Always wash your hands before handling food. Thoroughly wash all raw vegetables and fruits to remove dirt, chemicals, and insecticides. Wash uncooked poultry, fish, and meat under cold water.
- Use a cutting board when cutting up vegetables and fruits. Don't cut them up in your hand! And be sure to cut in a direction *away* from you and your fingers.
- Long hair or loose clothing can easily catch fire if brought near the burners of a stove. If you have long hair, tie it back before you start cooking.
- Turn all pot handles toward the back of the stove so that you will not catch your sleeves or jewelry on them. This is especially important when younger brothers and sisters are around. They could easily knock off a pot and get burned.
- Always use a pot holder to steady hot pots or to take pans out of the oven. Don't use a wet cloth on a hot pan because the steam it produces could burn you.
- Lift the lid of a steaming pot with the opening away from you so that you will not get burned.
- If you get burned, hold the burn under cold running water. Do not put grease or butter on it. Cold water helps to take the heat out, but grease or butter will only keep it in.
- If grease or cooking oil catches fire, throw baking soda or salt at the bottom of the flame to put it out. (Water will *not* put out a grease fire.) Call for help, and try to turn all the stove burners to "off."

Cooking Utensils

bamboo skewers—Long, thin bamboo sticks used for roasting pieces of food over hot coals

colander—A bowl with holes in the bottom and sides. It is used for washing food or draining liquid from a solid food.

Dutch oven—A heavy pot with a tight-fitting lid. Dutch ovens are often used for cooking soups or stews.

food processor—An electric appliance with a blade that revolves inside a container to chop, mix, or blend food

mortar—A strong bowl used with a pestle to grind, crush, or mash spices and other foods

pestle—A club-shaped utensil used with a mortar to grind, crush, or mash spices or other foods

slotted spoon—A spoon with small openings in the bowl, used to remove solid food from liquid

steamer—A covered pot with an insert something like a strainer, used for steaming vegetables

strainer—A small wire-mesh bowl with a handle. It is used to drain liquid from solid food or to remove solid bits from a liquid.

wok—A large, bowl-shaped pan that is used to stir-fry foods

Cooking Terms

beat—To stir rapidly in a circular motion

blanch—To submerge a food briefly in boiling water

boil—To heat a liquid over high heat until bubbles form and rise rapidly to the surface

broil—To cook food under a direct flame

brown—To cook food quickly over high heat so that the surface browns evenly

bruise—To crush food slightly, enabling more of the flavor to be released while cooking

core—To remove the core (the inedible central part) from a fruit

dice—To chop food into small, square pieces

garnish—To decorate a dish with small pieces of food, such as chopped parsley or slices of lime

grate—To shred food into tiny pieces by rubbing it against a grater

marinate—To soak food in a seasoned liquid in order to add flavor and tenderize it

mince—To chop food into very small pieces

preheat—To allow an oven to warm up to a certain temperature before putting food in it

sauté—To fry quickly in oil or fat, over high heat, stirring or turning the food to prevent burning

simmer—To cook over low heat in liquid kept just below its boiling point. Bubbles may occasionally rise to the surface.

steam—To cook food with the steam from boiling water

stir-fry—To quickly cook bite-sized pieces of food in a small amount of oil over high heat

zest—To scrape the peel from a lemon, lime, orange, or other citrus fruit using a cheese grater or a special utensil called a zester

Special Ingredients

Some of the following ingredients may be difficult to find at your local supermarket. Many of these foods are available at Asian markets. If you do not live near an Asian market, the Internet can be a great resource. Log on to <http://www.melroseflowers.com/mkic> for a list of Asian markets in your state and a list of shops that sell Asian ingredients over the Internet.

bay leaf—The dried leaf of the bay (also called laurel) tree, used to season food

bean sprouts—Edible sprouts, or young shoots, from the mung bean plant. Sprouts can be bought either canned or fresh, or you can grow your own.

bok choy—A type of cabbage with long, light green stems and deep green leaves, commonly used in stir-fries

bouillon—A broth typically made from spices, vegetables, and/or meat. Bouillon can be purchased in cans, as a powder, or in cubes.

candlenut (kemiri/tingkih)—A round, cream-colored seed with an oily consistency used to add texture and a mild flavor to many Indonesian dishes. If you can't find candlenuts, you can substitute macadamia nuts or raw cashews.

cellophane noodles—Thin, clear noodles made from mung beans

chayote—A green, pear-shaped squash

chives—A member of the onion family. The thin green shoots are chopped and used as a flavoring and a garnish.

coconut milk—The white, milky liquid extracted from coconut meat and used to give a coconut flavor to foods. It is available in cans at most grocery stores. Reduced-fat (light) coconut milk can be substituted for regular coconut milk in recipes.

coriander—The whole or ground seeds of the cilantro plant, used to season foods

crushed red pepper—The dried seeds and skin of a hot red pepper, used to make foods spicy

cumin—The seeds of an herb used whole or ground to give food a pungent, slightly hot flavor

egg noodles—Wide, flat pasta made from eggs and flour

gelatin—A clear, powdered substance used as a thickening agent

ginger—The knobby, light brown root of a tropical plant, used to flavor food. To use fresh ginger, slice off the amount called for, peel off the skin with the edge of a spoon, and grate the flesh. Freeze the rest of the root for future use. Fresh ginger has a very zippy taste, so use it sparingly. Do not substitute dried ground ginger in a recipe calling for fresh ginger, as the taste is very different.

grenadine—The sweet, concentrated juice of a pomegranate, or a pomegranate-flavored syrup, often used to flavor foods and drinks

kemiri nut—See *candlenut*

kunci root—A fibrous, spicy root related to ginger and used to flavor Indonesian dishes

lemongrass—A tropical grass, the thick blades of which are used to add a subtle lemon flavor

macadamia nuts—Round, hard nuts native to Australia that are grown commercially in Hawaii

peanut oil—Oil made from pressed peanuts that is used to stir-fry and deep-fry foods

raw peanuts—Peanuts that have not been roasted, salted, or flavored in any other way. Raw peanuts are often sold in bulk at grocery stores, food co-ops, and Asian markets.

rice wine vinegar—Vinegar made from rice wine

salam leaf (daun salam)—A subtly flavored leaf of the cassia family

sambal—See *Thai chili paste*

scallions—Another name for green onions

shallots—A member of the onion family, shallots are widely used in Indonesian cooking. They are peeled and pounded to make spice pastes, sliced and added to food before cooking, and sliced and deep-fried to make a garnish.

shrimp crackers—Small, Chinese-style crackers made from rice flour, wheat, or corn

shrimp paste—Bottled shrimp concentrate with a thick consistency

tamarind—The dark amber pulp of the fruit of the tamarind tree, an evergreen native to Asia. Tamarind can be purchased in pressed cakes and reconstituted with water.

Thai chili paste—A thick, spicy pepper sauce used to flavor Asian dishes

Thai fragrant (jasmine) rice—A short-grained white rice with a hint of sweet, spicy flavor that makes a great accompaniment to Indonesian dishes

tofu—A processed curd made from soybean milk. Tofu is available in the health food section of larger grocery stores and from food co-ops. Plain tofu tastes bland, but it absorbs flavor from other foods. It is a good source of protein.

turmeric—A yellow, aromatic spice made from the root of the turmeric plant

white wine vinegar—Vinegar made from white wine

zest—The very outer, brightly colored peel of citrus fruits such as lemons, limes, and oranges

Healthy and Low-Fat Cooking Tips

Indonesian cooking features many vegetarian dishes and entrées made with tofu or fresh fish. These foods are naturally low in fat and good for you.

There are many simple ways to reduce the fat content of most dishes. Following are a few general tips for adapting the recipes in this book. Throughout the book, you'll also find specific suggestions for individual recipes—and don't worry, they'll still taste delicious!

Many recipes call for butter or oil to sauté vegetables or other ingredients. Using oil lowers saturated fat, but you can also reduce the amount of oil you use. It's also a good idea to use a small, non-stick frying pan if you decide to use less oil than the recipe calls for. Or you can substitute a low-fat or nonfat cooking spray for oil.

Dairy products can be a source of unwanted fat. You can replace heavy cream with half-and-half and sweetened condensed milk with fat-free evaporated milk. Coconut milk, a common ingredient in Indonesian cooking, is high in fat, but you can use reduced-fat or "light" varieties.

Lamb, pork, chicken, and beef are used in Indonesian favorites such as sates and soups. Some cooks like to replace red meat with chicken, turkey, or chunks of tofu to lower the fat content. This does change the flavor, however. Buying extra-lean cuts of lamb, pork, or beef and trimming any visible fat are also easy ways to reduce fat.

Several Indonesian recipes call for soy sauce, a seasoning that, like salt, adds a great deal of flavor but is high in sodium. To lower the sodium content of these dishes, you may simply reduce the amount of soy sauce you use. You can also substitute low-sodium soy sauce. Soy sauce labeled "light" is usually lighter in color than regular soy sauce, not lower in sodium.

There are many ways to prepare meals that are good for you and still taste great. As you become a more experienced cook, try experimenting with recipes and substitutions to find the methods that work best for you.

METRIC CONVERSIONS

Cooks in the United States measure both liquid and solid ingredients using standard containers based on the 8-ounce cup and the tablespoon. These measurements are based on volume, while the metric system of measurement is based on both weight (for solids) and volume (for liquids). To convert from U.S. fluid tablespoons, ounces, quarts, and so forth to metric liters is a straightforward conversion, using the chart below. However, since solids have different weights—one cup of rice does not weigh the same as one cup of grated cheese, for example—many cooks who use the metric system have kitchen scales to weigh different ingredients. The chart below will give you a good starting point for basic conversions to the metric system.

MASS (weight)

1 ounce (oz.)	=	28.0 grams (g)
8 ounces	=	227.0 grams
1 pound (lb.) or 16 ounces	=	0.45 kilograms (kg)
2.2 pounds	=	1.0 kilogram

LIQUID VOLUME

1 teaspoon (tsp.)	=	5.0 milliliters (ml)
1 tablespoon (tbsp.)	=	15.0 milliliters
1 fluid ounce (oz.)	=	30.0 milliliters
1 cup (c.)	=	240 milliliters
1 pint (pt.)	=	480 milliliters
1 quart (qt.)	=	0.95 liters (l)
1 gallon (gal.)	=	3.80 liters

LENGTH

¼ inch (in.)	=	0.6 centimeters (cm)
½ inch	=	1.25 centimeters
1 inch	=	2.5 centimeters

TEMPERATURE

212°F	=	100°C (boiling point of water)
225°F	=	110°C
250°F	=	120°C
275°F	=	135°C
300°F	=	150°C
325°F	=	160°C
350°F	=	180°C
375°F	=	190°C
400°F	=	200°C

(To convert temperature in Fahrenheit to Celsius, subtract 32 and multiply by .56)

PAN SIZES

8-inch cake pan	=	20 x 4-centimeter cake pan
9-inch cake pan	=	23 x 3.5-centimeter cake pan
11 x 7-inch baking pan	=	28 x 18-centimeter baking pan
13 x 9-inch baking pan	=	32.5 x 23-centimeter baking pan
9 x 5-inch loaf pan	=	23 x 13-centimeter loaf pan
2-quart casserole	=	2-liter casserole

An Indonesian Table

At a traditional Indonesian dinner, the eating area is covered with many dishes. A large bowl of rice is always present, accompanied by several smaller bowls filled with a variety of side dishes, such as chicken or pork sate, vegetable soup, salad, and chicken in coconut cream sauce. Dutch colonists coined the term *De Rijstaffel* ("rice table") to describe this style of dining. In the countryside and small villages, a straw mat typically serves as a dinner table. Diners sit around the mat with their legs crossed.

An Indonesian who hosts a dinner for friends serves many different dishes so that the guests will have plenty to choose from. People take only the selections they want and leave the rest. Diners help themselves to rice and then try a little at a time from each dish. There is no silverware, as Indonesians prefer to use their fingers. But you will not see Indonesians lift food to their mouths with their left hand, since this hand is thought to be unclean. Guests always wait until the host indicates that it is OK to begin the meal before they taste anything. And they know not to finish everything on their plate—otherwise the host will keep serving them.

A Javanese family gathers for the evening meal. Like many Indonesians in rural areas, this group sits on a woven mat instead of dining at a table.

An Indonesian Menu

Rice, which grows abundantly in the island country's tropical climate, forms the basis of most Indonesian meals. Fresh fruits and vegetables, such as mangoes, bananas, coconuts, bean sprouts, green beans, and cabbage, served with beef, chicken, fish, or eggs, typically complete the meal. Favorite Indonesian dishes, such as gado-gado, fried rice, and sate, are seasoned with spices borrowed from the cuisines of neighboring countries such as China, India, and Thailand. Below are two Indonesian dinner menus, one vegetarian and one featuring chicken as the main course.

DINNER #1

Vegetable sour soup

Gado-gado

Vegetable sauté

Festive rice

Fried bananas

Most large supermarkets display a guide to the hotness of various types of chilies. If you're not used to eating spicy food, start with a mild chili such as Anaheim or poblano. The greatest heat is in the seeds and membranes.

SHOPPING LIST:

Produce

5 shallots
1 head garlic
1 inch-long piece fresh
 ginger
2 red chili peppers*
1 green chili pepper (optional)
1 chayote
2 medium onions
2½ c. green beans
2 medium red potatoes
1 c. bean sprouts
4 large carrots
2 medium cucumbers
2 heads green cabbage or 2
 bags shredded green
 cabbage
1 green bell pepper
2 stalks lemongrass
1 tomato
1 lime
4 small, ripe bananas

Dairy/Egg/Meat

2 eggs

Canned/Bottled/Boxed

shrimp paste
5 c. low-fat chicken or
 vegetable broth
peanut oil
soy sauce
canola oil
1 14-oz. can reduced-fat
 coconut milk
1 c. creamy, natural peanut
 butter

Miscellaneous

brown sugar
1 cake tamarind
1 8-oz. package frozen corn
 kernels
4 oz. package firm tofu
crushed red pepper
1 lb. Thai fragrant rice
salt
sugar
3 tbsp. (1 oz.) raw peanuts
½ c. (4 oz.) salted peanuts
turmeric
shrimp crackers
flour
1 bay leaf

DINNER #2

Balinese vegetable soup

Spicy fruit salad

Festive rice

Chicken in coconut cream sauce

Vanilla gelatin pudding

Produce

1 head garlic
4 medium shallots
1 c. bean sprouts
1 c. fresh green beans
   (frozen can be used if
   fresh aren't available)
1 chayote
1 Granny Smith apple
3 cucumbers
1 mango
1 orange
1 lime
4 stalks lemongrass
4 salam leaves
1 red chili pepper*
2 medium onions
1 tomato
1 inch-long piece fresh
   ginger

Dairy/Egg/Meat

1 pound (16 oz.) whole,
   boneless chicken breasts
1 quart milk

Canned/Bottled/Boxed

2 envelopes plain gelatin
lemon juice
3 14-oz. cans reduced-fat
   coconut milk
shrimp paste
canola oil
vegetable oil
1 14-oz. can diced pineapple
1 8-oz. can mandarin orange
   segments
vanilla extract

Miscellaneous

6 candlenuts or macadamia
   nuts or 12 almonds
ground coriander
salt
crushed red pepper
brown sugar (light or dark)
1 cake tamarind
1 lb. Thai fragrant rice
turmeric
shrimp crackers
sugar

Soups and Appetizers

Indonesian cooking includes a number of nutritious and satisfying soups that feature a delicious blend of chopped vegetables, tender bits of chicken, lamb, or beef, and sometimes coconut milk. Soups may be served in a variety of ways in Indonesia. Although soups are typically thought of as a first course, a steaming bowl can make a complete lunch or dinner on the go. Indonesians might stop for their midday meal at a warung to enjoy the soup of the day.

Appetizers such as corn fritters and beef sate tempt the taste buds, making diners hungry for the food that's yet to come. And, because of their smaller serving sizes, appetizers offer a great way to sample a variety of foods without filling up. Consider serving several appetizers to create a fun and varied meal.

Vegetable Sour Soup (recipe on page 34) and Corn Fritters (recipe on page 33) make a great duo. The earthy fritters set off the strong spices and flavors of the soup.

Balinese Vegetable Soup/Sayur Oelih

To make this soup a full meal, serve with a side of cooked rice (see recipe on page 44).

5 c. water

1 c. fresh green beans

1 clove garlic, minced

2 candlenuts or macadamia nuts or 4 almonds

½ tsp. shrimp paste

2 to 3 tsp. ground coriander

2 tbsp. vegetable oil

1 whole shallot, sliced thin

1 14-oz. can reduced-fat coconut milk

2 salam leaves*

1 c. bean sprouts

2 tbsp. lemon juice

½ tsp. salt

* If you can't find fresh or dried salam leaves, leave them out of the recipe.

1. In a large saucepan, bring water to a boil. Wash green beans and trim the ends. Carefully add beans to the boiling water and cook for about 4 minutes. Use a slotted spoon to remove beans from the water and transfer them to a separate bowl. Save the bean cooking water.

2. Using a mortar and pestle, food processor, or blender, grind garlic, nuts, shrimp paste, and coriander to make a paste.

3. In a Dutch oven or large saucepan, heat vegetable oil and add the shallot. Fry over medium heat until transparent, then use a slotted spoon to transfer shallot to a small bowl.

4. Add spice paste to the Dutch oven and stir-fry for about 2 minutes. Add bean cooking water, coconut milk, and salam leaves. Bring to a boil. Reduce the heat and cook uncovered for about 20 minutes.

5. Before serving, add green beans, shallot, bean sprouts, and lemon juice and stir gently. Add ½ tsp. salt, stir, and serve.

Preparation time: 20 minutes
Cooking time: 35 minutes
Serves 8

Corn Fritters / Perkedel Jagung

Indonesians eat corn fritters plain or dip them in sambal, a spicy sauce made with fresh red hot peppers. Look for jars of sambal or Thai chili paste at your local grocery store or Asian market.

Spice paste:

1 tbsp. kunci root, pounded with mortar and pestle*

2 tsp. ground coriander

1 tsp. freshly ground pepper

6 shallots, peeled and chopped fine

3 garlic cloves, minced

1 tsp. salt

1 tbsp. sugar

Fritters:

2½ c. frozen or fresh corn, cut from the cob

1 tbsp. chives, finely chopped

1 egg, beaten

2 tbsp. flour

1 c. canola oil for frying

1. To make the spice paste, combine all ingredients in a medium bowl. Set aside.

2. Grind corn kernels in a food processor or blender.

3. Scrape corn into a large mixing bowl and add chives, egg, flour, and spice paste. Mix with a wooden spoon or electric mixer to make a smooth, thick batter.

4. In a large, heavy frying pan, heat oil over medium-high heat. When a bit of batter dropped into the pan sizzles immediatcly, the oil is ready for frying. To make a fritter, use a large mixing spoon to carefully drop 2 tbsp. of batter into the pan. Fry fritter for 2 to 4 minutes, or until it turns golden brown. You may make up to four fritters at a time. When they are done, use a spatula to transfer them to a plate covered with a paper towel. Serve hot with sambal or Thai chili sauce.

* Kunci root is in the same family as ginger and can be found at Asian markets. If you can't find kunci root, substitute fresh ginger.

Preparation time: 25 minutes
Cooking time: 20 minutes
Serves 5 or 6

Vegetable Sour Soup / Sayur Asam

This is one of the most popular soups in Indonesia. When served as part of a larger meal, it usually accompanies Javanese-style fried chicken and steamed rice.

1 tsp. tamarind

5 tbsp. warm water

1 shallot, sliced

3 cloves garlic, minced

1 inch-long piece fresh ginger, peeled and sliced

1 red chili pepper, seeded and sliced*

3 tbsp. raw peanuts

1 tsp. shrimp paste

½ tsp. salt

5 c. low-fat chicken or vegetable broth

½ c. salted peanuts, coarsely chopped

2 tbsp. brown sugar

1 chayote, peeled, seeded, and sliced thin

½ c. fresh or frozen green beans, ends trimmed

⅓ c. frozen corn kernels

1 green chili pepper, sliced (optional)

*Always wear rubber or latex gloves when working with chili peppers. To seed the chili, slit it lengthwise with a sharp paring knife and remove the seeds with a spoon or the tip of a vegetable peeler.

1. Prepare tamarind by placing it in a small bowl with warm water. Let soak for 15 minutes.

2. To make spice paste, combine shallot, garlic, ginger, red chili pepper, raw peanuts, shrimp paste, and salt in a large mortar and blend well with a pestle. Use a food processor or blender if you don't have a mortar and pestle.

3. Transfer paste to a medium saucepan and add chicken or vegetable broth, salted peanuts, and brown sugar. Stir to combine, and cook over medium heat for 15 minutes.

4. Meanwhile, use a strainer to separate the tamarind seeds from the juice. Throw away the seeds and keep the juice.

5. Add chayote, green beans, and corn to the soup, and cook over high heat for 5 minutes.

6. Just before serving, add tamarind juice and stir. Garnish with green chili pepper slices if desired.

Preparation time: 25 minutes
Cooking time: 20 minutes
Serves 4

Sweet and Sour Beef Sate with Peanut Sauce/
Sate Daging Sapi Manis Pedas Sambal Kacang

Sate—skewered pieces of beef or chicken cooked over hot coals—is a popular snack and appetizer in Indonesia. This recipe is for beef sate, but you can easily substitute chicken. Typically, the meat is served with a spicy peanut sauce called **sambal kacang.**

Sate

2 tsp. ground coriander

¼ tsp. ground cumin

2 cloves garlic, minced

1 tsp. salt

1 tbsp. brown sugar

1 tsp. tamarind, dissolved in 1 tbsp. warm water

1 lb. sirloin steak, cut into 1-inch cubes

2 tbsp. soy sauce

1 tbsp. water

1 tbsp. peanut oil

bamboo skewers*

1. With a mortar and pestle, food processor, or blender, combine coriander, cumin, garlic, salt, brown sugar, and tamarind.

2. Place steak cubes in a medium bowl and add the spice mixture. Use your fingers to rub the spices into the meat. Set meat in the refrigerator and marinate for 1 hour.

3. In a wide, shallow dish, mix soy sauce, water, and peanut oil.

4. Place four pieces of marinated meat on each skewer and dip the meat into the soy sauce mixture.

5. Broil meat over a charcoal fire or under the broiler of the oven. Cook for 3 minutes on each side. Serve with peanut sauce (recipe on following page).

Preparation time: 25 minutes
Cooking time: 10 minutes
Marinating time: 1 hour
Serves 4

* To prevent the bamboo skewers from burning, soak them in water for 1 hour before using.

Peanut Sauce:

1 tbsp. peanut oil

1 clove garlic, minced

1 c. water

1 tsp. crushed red pepper

2 tsp. tamarind, dissolved in 2 tbsp.
  warm water

½ tsp. salt

2 tbsp. sugar

¼ tsp. shrimp paste

1 c. creamy, natural peanut butter
  (available at most food co-ops)

1. Heat oil in a frying pan over medium-high heat. Add garlic and cook for 1 minute.

2. Add water, crushed red pepper, tamarind, salt, sugar, and shrimp paste. Cook for 5 minutes.

3. Add peanut butter and stir until combined. Simmer for 5 minutes, stirring often and adding a tablespoon of water if the mixture becomes too thick.

4. Serve warm or hot with sate.

Preparation time: 15 minutes
Makes 1 cup

Salads and Side Dishes

The abundance of fresh fruits and vegetables in Indonesia makes for especially delicious salads and side dishes. Indonesians who live in the city can shop every day at indoor farmers' markets for a variety of just-picked bananas, mangoes, jackfruit, coconuts, tomatoes, sweet potatoes, and cucumbers. In rural areas and small villages, fresh produce is available at outdoor markets once a week, but most people grow their own fruits and vegetables.

Gado-gado, a salad made from potatoes, green beans, bean sprouts, broccoli, celery, and carrots and topped with a peanut dressing, is a favorite dish throughout the islands. Gado-gado can be a meal in itself. Lighter salads, such as carrot and apple salad or tomato, cucumber, and onion salad, provide a sweet, cool accompaniment to spicy main entrées. Serving three or four salads together makes a great meal on a hot summer day.

A salad that is hearty enough to be a meal in itself, gado-gado is popular in all parts of Indonesia. (Recipe on pages 40–41.)

Gado-Gado

This classic Indonesian salad is very easy to make. Feel free to substitute other vegetables you may have on hand for some of the ones listed here. Yams can be a tasty substitution for red potatoes, and peeled broccoli stalks can stand in for green beans.

1 c. red potatoes (about 2 medium potatoes)

1 c. fresh green beans, ends trimmed

2 c. green cabbage, shredded

1 c. fresh bean sprouts

1 c. carrots (1 to 1½ carrots), peeled and thinly sliced

1 c. cucumber (about 1 medium cucumber), sliced

2 tbsp. canola oil

4 oz. firm tofu, cut into 1-inch cubes

2 hard-boiled eggs, peeled*

deep-fried shallots for garnish**

peanut sauce (recipe on page 37)

1. Fill a large saucepan with water and bring to a boil. Use a slotted spoon to carefully lower the potatoes into the water. Cook for about 20 minutes, or until the potatoes can be pierced easily with a fork. Then use the slotted spoon to transfer the potatoes to a colander. Rinse under cold water. When cool enough to handle, slice the potatoes.

2. Fill a second saucepan with water and bring to a boil. Use a slotted spoon to lower the green beans into the water. Cook for about 3 minutes. Use the slotted spoon to move the blanched beans to a colander. Rinse under cold water.

3. One vegetable at a time, repeat this procedure to blanch the cabbage, bean sprouts, and carrots.

4. Arrange green beans, cabbage, bean sprouts, carrots, potatoes, and cucumbers however you like on a large platter and set aside.

5. Heat oil in a skillet over medium heat. Cook tofu cubes for about 10 minutes, or until crisp and lightly browned. Remove from the pan and drain on paper towels. Scatter tofu cubes over the salad.

6. Cut hard-boiled eggs into quarters and arrange along the edge of the platter. Serve gado-gado with fried shallots (see below) and peanut sauce (recipe on page 37).

Preparation time: 20 minutes
Cooking time: 45 minutes
Serves 6

*To make hard-boiled eggs, fill a medium saucepan with water and bring to a boil. Use a slotted spoon to lower eggs into the water one at a time. Boil eggs for 10 minutes, then use the slotted spoon to remove them from the water. Transfer eggs to a clean plate. Allow the eggs to cool completely before removing the shells.

**To make deep-fried shallots, cut 1 shallot into thin slices and sprinkle with ½ tsp. salt. Heat ½ c. canola oil in a skillet and fry the shallots 5 to 7 minutes, stirring frequently. When the shallots brown slightly, remove from pan and drain on paper towels.

Spicy Fruit Salad / Rujak

1 chayote, peeled

1 Granny Smith apple, cored

2 cucumbers, peeled and cut in half
lengthwise with seeds removed*

1 mango**

1 orange, peeled and divided into
sections

½ tsp. crushed red pepper

¼ tsp. shrimp paste

3 tbsp. brown sugar

½ tsp. salt

1 tsp. tamarind, dissolved in 1 tbsp.
warm water

1 14-oz. can diced pineapple,
drained

1. Coarsely chop chayote, apple,
cucumbers, mango, and orange
sections.

2. In a large bowl, combine crushed
red pepper, shrimp paste, brown
sugar, salt, and tamarind to make a
paste.

3. Add chayote, apple, cucumber,
mango, orange, and pineapple to
the bowl, and stir well to combine.
Serve at room temperature.

Preparation time: 25 minutes
Serves 6

*An easy way to remove the seeds from a cucumber is to use the tip of
a vegetable peeler to scrape them out.

**To peel and cut a mango, set the fruit on a cutting board so that the ridge that
covers the pit is face-up. Using a sharp knife, carefully make two cuts on either side of this
ridge (parallel to the ridge), slicing through the fruit. Discard the pit and place the two halves
on the cutting board, skin side down. Use the knife to score the flesh of these two halves,
creating a checkerboard pattern. Taking each half in your hand, push up in the center from the
skin side to loosen the scored cubes of mango from the skin. Carefully slide the knife
between the cubes and the mango skin to cut them from the fruit.

Carrot and Apple Salad / Selada Bortel

1 Granny Smith apple, cored and
    cut into quarters

3 tbsp. lemon juice

1 tbsp. canola oil

1 tsp. sugar

3 large carrots, washed and peeled

½ tsp. salt

½ tsp. pepper

1. Using a cheese grater, grate apple, including the skin, into a medium bowl. Sprinkle with lemon juice and use your hands to combine thoroughly.

2. Add oil and sugar to grated apple.

3. Grate carrots over a medium bowl. Add grated carrots, salt, and pepper to apple mixture. Mix.

4. Cover and store in the refrigerator until ready to serve.

Preparation time: 15 minutes
Serves 6

Thai Fragrant (Jasmine) Rice / Nasi Wangi Thailand

1 c. Thai fragrant rice

2 c. water

1. Combine rice and water in medium saucepan.

2. Bring to a boil, cover the pan, and reduce heat to a simmer.

3. Cook for about 20 minutes. Fluff with a fork and serve immediately.

Preparation time: 20 minutes
Makes 2 cups

Tomato, Cucumber, and Onion Salad / Acar Ketimun

1 cucumber, washed well

1 tomato, skin and seeds removed, diced*

1 small onion, cut into thin slices

3 tbsp. rice wine vinegar or white wine vinegar

2 tsp. sugar

1 red chili pepper, seeded and chopped**

pinch of salt

1. With a vegetable peeler, remove strips of skin from cucumber lengthwise, leaving some of the skin intact to add color to the salad. Cut the ends from the cucumber and discard. Cut cucumber into thin slices.

2. Arrange cucumber, diced tomato, and sliced onion in rows in a large, shallow bowl, and set aside.

3. In a small bowl, combine vinegar, sugar, chili pepper, and a pinch of salt. Pour the mixture over the vegetables.

4. Cover and chill until ready to serve.

Preparation time: 25 minutes
Serves 6

*To peel a tomato, cut a small x in the skin at the top and bottom. Place tomato in a small saucepan of boiling water for about 30 seconds. Remove tomato with a slotted spoon and cool until it is warm but no longer hot. Use a small paring knife to peel off the skin. It will come off easily. To seed a tomato, cut the peeled tomato in half and gently squeeze it over the kitchen sink.

** See tip on page 34 about seeding and cutting chilies.

Main Dishes

Although many Indonesian recipes call for lamb or beef, most Indonesians cannot afford these meats on a day-to-day basis. Instead, main dishes tend to center on fish or chicken, which are readily available and much less expensive there. To make the most of a small amount of meat, cooks often cut it into bite-sized pieces, mix it with vegetables, and serve it with rice. Duck and pork dishes are favored in parts of the islands with large Chinese-Indonesian populations, but pork is not eaten in areas where most people are Muslim.

Delicious vegetarian dishes abound in Indonesia. Tofu and vegetables are used instead of meat in many dishes to cut costs. And if an entrée does contain meat, there are always plenty of other vegetable and rice dishes from which to build a nutritious meal. The following section includes one vegetarian main dish. If you choose, you can easily make the other main dishes vegetarian by substituting a variety of vegetables or tofu for the meat.

The rich but mild flavors of Stir-Fried Noodles with Shrimp (recipe on page 50) blend well with the refreshing Tomato, Cucumber, and Onion Salad (recipe on page 45), creating a light yet satisfying meal.

Soy Sauce Fish/Ikan Kecap

Indonesian cooking includes many recipes for seafood. This recipe calls for types of fish that are available fresh or frozen the world over, so even landlubbers can partake.

1 lb. mackerel, cod, or haddock
  fillets

1 tsp. salt

2 tbsp. flour

3 tbsp. peanut oil

½ tsp. shrimp paste

2 tbsp. water

1 medium onion, coarsely chopped

1 large clove garlic, minced

1 ½ inch-long piece fresh ginger,
  peeled and finely chopped

1 red chili, seeded and chopped*

3 tbsp. lemon juice

1 tbsp. brown sugar

2 to 4 tbsp. soy sauce

4 large lettuce leaves

* See tip on page 34 about
seeding and cutting chilies.

1. Wash fish under cold water and pat dry with paper towels. Cut fillets into 2 x 3-inch pieces.

2. In a shallow bowl or pie plate, use a fork to mix salt and flour. One by one, roll fish fillets in the flour and set on a clean plate.

3. Heat 2 tbsp. of the peanut oil in a skillet and fry fish for 3 to 4 minutes per side. Place on a plate, cover with foil to keep warm, and set aside.

4. In a small bowl, mix together shrimp paste and 2 tbsp. water.

5. Clean and dry the skillet before heating the remaining 1 tbsp. peanut oil. Add onion, garlic, ginger, and chili pepper and stir-fry for about 5 minutes.

6. Add shrimp paste to the onion mixture and cook for 2 minutes. Add lemon juice, brown sugar, and soy sauce to taste. Stir to combine.

7. Arrange lettuce leaves on four plates and place fish on top. Pour the sauce over the fish and serve.

Preparation time: 20 minutes
Cooking time: 20 minutes
Serves 4

Stir-Fried Noodles with Shrimp/*Bakmi Goreng*

5 c. water

1 lb. egg noodles

3 tbsp. peanut oil

¼ c. onion (about ½ medium onion), thinly sliced

2 cloves garlic, minced

1 lb. peeled, deveined shrimp*

2 tbsp. soy sauce

½ c. celery leaves and small stems, chopped into ½-inch pieces

3 scallions, chopped

3 c. bok choy, chopped

1 tsp. salt

½ tsp. pepper

1. In a large saucepan, bring water to a boil. Add noodles and cook for 3 minutes, stirring often.

2. Drain noodles and immediately rinse with cold water. Combine noodles with 1 tbsp. peanut oil and set aside.

3. In a mortar and pestle, blender, or food processor, combine 2 tbsp. onion and the garlic to make a paste.

4. Heat the remaining 2 tbsp. oil in a wok or skillet and add the rest of the onion. Add shrimp and stir-fry for 2 minutes.

5. Add soy sauce, celery, scallions, bok choy, salt, and pepper and fry for another 2 minutes.

6. Add noodles to the mixture. Stir-fry for 2 more minutes, until all of the ingredients are combined and heated. Serve hot or at room temperature.

Preparation time: 30 minutes
Cooking time: 10 minutes
Serves 4

*To make this a vegetarian entrée, replace the shrimp with 1½ c. trimmed green beans and ½ c. chopped red bell pepper.

Vegetable Sauté/ Oseng Sayuran

You can substitute other vegetables, such as celery or broccoli, for the vegetables called for in this recipe.

1 tsp. crushed red pepper

1 tsp. salt

½ tsp. sugar

1 bay leaf

1 tbsp. soy sauce

2 tbsp. peanut oil

¼ c. shallot (1 or 2 whole shallots), thinly sliced

2 cloves garlic, minced

2 c. green cabbage, shredded

1 c. green beans, ends trimmed

½ c. green pepper, chopped

1 c. carrots (1 to 2 carrots), thinly sliced

1. In a small bowl, combine crushed red pepper, salt, sugar, bay leaf, and soy sauce. Set aside.

2. Heat oil in a skillet or wok over medium-high heat and add shallot and garlic. Stir-fry for 2 minutes.

3. Add cabbage, beans, green pepper, carrots, and the soy sauce mixture and stir-fry for about 6 minutes. The vegetables should still be crunchy—be careful not to overcook. Serve hot with rice.

Preparation time: 20 minutes
Cooking time: 15 minutes
Serves 4

Chicken in Coconut Cream Sauce / *Opor Ayam*

1 16-oz. package whole, boneless chicken breasts, rinsed, patted dry, and cut into 1 x 2-inch pieces*

½ tsp. salt

1 shallot, chopped

4 cloves garlic, minced

4 candlenuts or macadamia nuts, or 8 almonds

1 tsp. ground coriander

3 tbsp. canola oil

1 inch-long piece ginger, peeled and minced

2 stalks lemongrass, bruised

1 tsp. lime zest

2 salam leaves

1 tsp. sugar

1 14-oz. can reduced-fat coconut milk

1 tsp. salt

2 cups cooked Thai fragrant rice (see recipe p. 44)

1. Preheat oven to 375°F. Season chicken pieces with about ½ tsp. salt, place in an oiled roasting pan, and bake for 25 to 30 minutes.

2. While the chicken bakes, use a mortar and pestle, blender, or food processor to grind shallot, garlic, nuts, and coriander to a fine paste.

3. Heat canola oil in a wok or skillet over medium-high heat and stir-fry the paste for about 3 minutes. Do not allow it to brown.

4. Remove chicken from oven. Add the chicken pieces, ginger, lemongrass, lime zest, salam leaves, sugar, coconut milk, and salt to wok. Stir well to coat chicken evenly with sauce.

5. Bring chicken mixture to a boil, then reduce the heat. Simmer uncovered for 30 to 40 minutes, or until sauce is thick. Stir every 5 to 10 minutes.

6. Before serving, remove lemongrass stalks. Serve chicken over rice.

Preparation time: 30 minutes
Cooking time: 1 hour
Serves 4

After handling raw chicken or other poultry, always remember to thoroughly wash your hands, utensils, and preparation area with soapy hot water. Also, when checking chicken for doneness, it's a good idea to cut it open gently to make sure that the meat is white (not pink) all the way through.

Desserts

Indonesia's steamy climate makes light, fruity desserts more appealing than rich, decadent treats such as cake or pie. After a large meal, Indonesians typically reach for fresh fruit such as mangoes, jackfruit, or bananas. But some favorite desserts are served on special occasions or when guests come to dinner. Black rice pudding, sweet coconut-rice balls, and steamed coconut custard are likely to appear on holiday tables. These sweets feature foods that grow in abundance on the islands, including bananas, coconuts, and rice. Some desserts, such as deep-fried bananas, can be purchased from street vendors to eat as a sweet snack in the sweltering heat of the afternoon.

Fried Bananas are prepared in various ways in cultures throughout the world. Indonesians garnish them with lime juice and a sprinkle of sugar. (Recipe on page 56.)

Fried Bananas/ Pisang Goreng

The key to melt-in-your-mouth fried bananas is to cook them immediately before serving so that the crust is crisp and the fruit is soft and warm.

¾ c. flour

½ tsp. salt

¾ to 1 c. water

1 lime, zested and cut into wedges

4 small, ripe bananas

1 c. canola oil for frying

1 tbsp. sugar

1. In a medium bowl, combine flour and salt.

2. Add enough water to make a smooth batter that is somewhat thick. Add lime zest and mix well.

3. Peel bananas and dip them in the batter 2 or 3 times, until well coated.

4. In a deep skillet, heat oil to 375°F, or until a piece of bread browns in 30 seconds.*

5. Place bananas in the oil slowly and carefully. Fry two at a time, until they are crisp and golden brown. Remove with a slotted spoon and place on paper towels to absorb the oil.

6. To serve, arrange bananas on a plate and sprinkle with sugar. Garnish with lime wedges.

Preparation time: 10 minutes
Cooking time: 10 minutes
Serves 4

*Do not cook with hot oil unless an adult is present. Use a fat thermometer to check the temperature of the oil.

Vanilla Gelatin Pudding/*Puding Vanila*

2 envelopes plain gelatin powder

4 c. milk

1 tbsp. sugar

1 tsp. vanilla extract

½ c. canned mandarin orange
    segments

1. Follow directions on the package to dissolve the gelatin.

2. In a separate pan, combine milk, sugar, and vanilla and bring to a boil, stirring frequently.

3. Remove from heat and add gelatin and mandarin orange slices, stirring until the mixture begins to thicken.

4. Fill a gelatin mold or medium bowl with cold water and allow to chill for 5 minutes. Pour out the water and fill the mold or bowl with the gelatin mixture. Refrigerate overnight or until firm.

5. If you used a gelatin mold, remove the pudding before serving. Set the mold in a sink or large bowl of warm water for about 5 minutes (make sure that the water level is just below the top of the mold). Remove the mold from the water and place a serving plate facedown over the top of the mold. Carefully flip so that the plate is on the bottom and the mold on top. Lift the mold. If you made the pudding in a bowl, serve as is.

Preparation time: 30 minutes
Chilling time: overnight
Serves 6

Potato Snowball Cookies/*Kue Bola*

5 large red potatoes, peeled

2 tbsp. flour

2 eggs

½ tsp. salt

½ tsp. vanilla extract

½ c. sugar

2 tbsp. milk

I c. canola oil

I c. powdered sugar

1. Boil the potatoes for 20 minutes, or until they can be easily pierced with a fork. Drain. Use a potato masher or fork to mash the potatoes. Set aside and allow to cool completely.

2. In a large mixing bowl, combine flour, eggs, salt, vanilla, sugar, and milk. Stir in the mashed potatoes.

3. Shape mixture into 1-inch balls and place on a clean plate.

4. Heat oil in a wok or large skillet over high heat. The oil is hot enough when a pinch of the potato mixture quickly sizzles to a golden brown. Use a slotted spoon to carefully lower a few of the potato balls at a time into the hot oil. Cook until golden brown, about 7 to 10 minutes.

5. Remove balls from oil and place on paper towels to cool. Sprinkle with powdered sugar before serving.

Preparation time: 30 minutes
Cooking time: 30 minutes
Makes 1 dozen cookies

Steamed Coconut Custard / Kue Talam Kelapa

3 eggs*

1 14-oz. can reduced-fat coconut
milk

5 tbsp. water

3 tbsp. sugar

1 oz. cellophane noodles, soaked in
warm water for 5 minutes

4 ripe bananas, peeled and chopped

1 tsp. salt

vanilla ice cream or frozen yogurt

1. In a medium bowl, beat eggs. Add coconut milk, water, and sugar. Stir to combine.

2. Pour egg mixture into a 2-quart casserole dish.

3. Meanwhile, drain cellophane noodles and chop into small pieces.

4. Add noodles, bananas, and salt to the egg mixture and mix well.

5. Cover the casserole dish with aluminum foil and place in a steamer for about 1 hour. If you do not have a steamer, fill a large rectangular cake pan with ½ inch of water. Place the casserole dish in the center of the cake pan and cover the entire thing with foil. Place in a preheated 350°F oven and bake for 45 minutes to 1 hour. The custard is done when a knife inserted in the center comes out clean.

6. Serve hot or cold with vanilla ice cream or frozen yogurt.

*To reduce the cholesterol content
of this dish, use egg substitute
instead of real eggs.

Preparation time: 15 minutes
Cooking time: 45 minutes to 1 hour
Serves 8

Holiday and Festival Foods

Rice, a mainstay of everyday cuisine in Indonesia, is the center of holiday and festival meals as well. On Lebaran, the celebration that brings an end to the fasting of Ramadan, festive rice molded into a cone is the centerpiece of the holiday table. Street vendors sell *ketupat*, rice cakes wrapped in palm leaves. On other holidays, such as Galungan, rice is placed in front of altars as an offering to the gods. On Maulud Nabi, a holiday honoring the birth of Muhammad, the prophet and founder of Islam, worshippers carry mounds of rice and fresh fruit in a parade. The rice is blessed and divided among festivalgoers. The rice harvest itself is also a cause for celebration. The very first bull race of Madura took place in a rice field after the crop had been harvested.

The recipes that follow are dishes that are enjoyed during Indonesian holidays, festivals, or special occasions. In the spirit of an Indonesian celebration, invite a group of friends over to sample these delights.

Pork Sate (recipe on page 66) is marinated for extra zest and served with a spicy peanut sauce (recipe on page 37).

Festive Rice/Nasi Kuning

The turmeric in this recipe tints the rice a fun, bright yellow hue.

4 tbsp. canola oil

2 cloves garlic, minced

2 medium onions, chopped fine

1 tbsp. turmeric

1 lb. uncooked Thai fragrant rice

3 c. water

1 14-oz. can reduced-fat coconut milk

2 stalks lemongrass

1 tsp. salt

1 red chili pepper, seeded and chopped

1 medium cucumber, peeled and sliced thickly

1 tomato, cut into wedges

deep-fried shallots (see tip on p. 41)

10 fried shrimp crackers*

1. In a Dutch oven, heat oil over medium heat. Add garlic, onions, and turmeric and stir-fry for 3 minutes, until onions are soft but not brown.

2. Add rice and stir to coat.

3. Add water, coconut milk, lemongrass, and salt. Bring mixture to a boil, stirring frequently.

4. Cover, reduce heat, and simmer for about 20 minutes, or until the rice has absorbed all of the liquid.

5. Remove from heat and cover pan with a dish towel. Set aside for 15 minutes.

6. Remove lemongrass stalks. Mound the rice on a serving platter. Garnish with chili pepper, cucumber, tomato, fried shallots, and shrimp crackers.

Preparation time: 45 minutes
Cooking time: 30 minutes
Serves 4 to 6

*To fry shrimp crackers, cover the bottom of a large skillet with ½ inch canola oil. Heat oil to 375°F, or until a cube of bread browns in 30 seconds. Carefully place shrimp crackers in the oil one by one. Cook until each cracker expands and becomes puffy. Use a slotted spoon to remove each cracker from oil before cracker begins to brown. Drain crackers on paper towels.

Pork Sate/ Sate Babi

Pork sate is a popular festival food on the island of Bali.

1¼ lb. pork loin, cut into 1-inch cubes

bamboo skewers (see tip on p. 36)

Marinade:

½ c. soy sauce

3 cloves garlic, minced

3 tbsp. peanut oil

½ c. raw peanuts, chopped

½ tsp. salt

½ tsp. pepper

Dipping sauce:

1 medium shallot, chopped fine

2 red chili peppers, seeded and
    chopped

½ c. soy sauce

6 tbsp. water

5 tbsp. lime juice

½ c. unsalted peanuts, chopped

Garnish:

lime wedges

deep-fried shallots
    (See tip on page 41)

1. In a medium bowl, combine soy sauce, garlic, peanut oil, raw peanuts, salt, and pepper to make the marinade. Add meat cubes to the marinade and place the bowl in the refrigerator for 1 hour or more. Stir meat from time to time.

2. Slide the marinated meat onto skewers and place on a clean plate.

3. Make dipping sauce by combining shallot, chili peppers, soy sauce, and water in a medium saucepan. Bring mixture to a boil, then reduce heat and simmer for about 5 minutes. Turn off the heat and allow sauce to cool before adding lime juice. Set aside.

4. Meanwhile, preheat the broiler or grill and broil sates, turning frequently. Cook for 5 to 8 minutes, or until tender.

5. Serve sates on a large platter and garnish with lime wedges and deep-fried shallots. Add peanuts to the sauce and pour the mixture into a bowl just before serving.

Preparation time: 15 minutes
Marinating time: 1 hour
Cooking time: 15 minutes
Makes about 15 skewers

Curried Java Soup/ *Sayur Kare*

Curried meat dishes, such as this savory soup, are typically served during Ramadan after the sun sets.

1 lb. beef stew meat, cut into bite-sized pieces*

4 c. water

3 beef or chicken bouillon cubes

2 tbsp. butter**

4 scallions, chopped

2 cloves garlic, minced

1 red chili pepper, minced

1 tbsp. ground dried ginger

1 tsp. turmeric

1 tbsp. ground coriander

½ tsp. ground cumin

1 tsp. shrimp paste

1 stalk lemongrass

1 salam leaf

1 c. diced fresh or frozen green beans

5 small red potatoes, peeled and chopped

1 c. reduced-fat coconut milk

½ tsp. sugar

1. In a Dutch oven, combine beef, water, and bouillon cubes and bring to a boil. Reduce heat and simmer for 1 hour.

2. While meat is cooking, heat butter in a wok or skillet over medium-high heat. Add scallions, garlic, chili pepper, ginger, turmeric, coriander, cumin, and shrimp paste and cook for 5 minutes.

3. Add lemongrass and salam leaf and cook for 2 more minutes.

4. Add spice mixture to the beef stock and simmer for 5 minutes.

5. Stir in green beans and potatoes. Cover and cook for 10 minutes.

6. Add coconut milk and sugar. Cook uncovered for 5 minutes, or until the vegetables are tender. Serve hot.

Preparation time: 30 minutes
Cooking time: 1 hour 30 minutes
Serves 6

*Other meats may be used in place of the beef if you prefer. To make this a vegetarian dish, substitute fried tofu cubes for the beef and vegetable bouillon cubes in place of beef or chicken bouillon. Add the tofu cubes at the very end and allow to cook for 10 minutes, or until the tofu is heated through.

**To reduce the saturated fat in this recipe, use canola oil or peanut oil in place of the butter.

Indonesian Ice Drink/ *Es Campur*

This beverage is a favorite in Indonesia and is often sold by street vendors at festivals. The drink's colorful, varied ingredients give it a very festive look and taste.

1 package gelatin dessert, any flavor

5 ice cubes per person

1 14-oz. can pineapple chunks, cut into small cubes

3 tbsp. canned corn, drained and washed

3 tbsp. canned kidney beans, drained and washed

1 14-oz. can coconut segments, cut into small pieces*

1 14-oz. can mandarin orange segments, drained, washed, and cut into small pieces

1 mango, cut into small pieces*

grenadine, snow cone syrup, or cherry-flavored Italian soda syrup

1 14-oz. can reduced-fat sweetened condensed milk

1. Make gelatin in a medium casserole pan, according to the package instructions. When it's firm, cut into small cubes.

2. Grind ice cubes in a blender until well crushed and divide ice evenly into three to six glasses, depending on how many servings you want.

3. Into each glass, sprinkle 1 tbsp. gelatin cubes, 1 tbsp. pineapple pieces, 1 tsp. corn, 1 tsp. kidney beans, 1 tbsp. coconut segments, 1 tbsp. mandarin orange segments, and 1 tbsp. mango pieces.

4. Top each glass with ¼ cup grenadine or syrup and ¼ cup sweetened condensed milk. Stir. Serve with a straw and spoon.

Preparation time: 30 minutes
Cooling time: 3 hours to cool gelatin
Serves 3 to 6 people

*Look for cans of coconut segments in Asian grocery stores.

** See tip on page 42 for instructions on how to cut a mango.

Index

About the Authors

Kari Cornell is an avid cook who loves to experiment with new recipes and cuisines. As an editor and coauthor of children's books for several years, Kari is pleased to combine the two activities she enjoys most to write *Cooking the Indonesian Way*.

Merry Anwar enjoys cooking and baking. She obtained a business degree at the University of Kansas and went on to earn a master's degree in finance from Golden Gate University in San Francisco. Merry owns and operates a flower shop called Melrose Flowers in Jakarta, Indonesia. Her dream is to open her own restaurant someday. Her website, <http//www.melroseflowers.com/mkic>, is a great resource for those interested in Indonesian cuisine.

Photo Acknowledgments
The photographs in this book are reproduced with the permission of:
© Michele Burgess, pp. 2–3, 11; © Walter and Louiseann Pietrowicz/September 8th Stock, pp. 4 (all), 5 (all), 6, 16, 30, 35, 38, 43, 46, 49, 53, 54, 58, 61, 62, 65, 68; © Lindsay Hebberd/CORBIS, p. 14; © Dean Conger/CORBIS, p. 26.

Cover photos: Walter and Louiseann Pietrowicz/September 8th Stock

The illustrations on pages 7, 17, 27, 31, 32, 33, 34, 36, 39, 41 (both), 42 (both), 45 (both), 47, 48, 50, 52, 55, 56, 60, 63, 64, 67, and 69 are by Tim Seeley. The map on page 8 is by Bill Hauser.